Echoes Of The Inner Voice

Where Silence Speaks and Heartbeats Write

Nisa

BookLeaf Publishing

India | USA | UK

Made with ❤ on the BookLeaf Publishing Platform
www.bookleafpub.in
www.bookleafpub.com

Dedication

"To my younger self, who once lacked confidence in speaking and found solace in penning down thoughts to express feelings—writing became the calm to my overthinking mind.

To my loving partner, for always supporting and believing in me.

To my parents on both sides, one who nurtured my capabilities and the other who never stopped believing in me.

And last but not least, to my dear sister, whose presence I've always felt, even when I merely thought of her.

This is my heartfelt dedication for Echoes of Inner Voice."

Preface

Echoes of the Inner Voice is a collection of poems I have been writing over the years. It reflects my thoughts and emotions as I see the world around me. At first, I thought my way of thinking was silly—that my thoughts were just random and not important. I used to feel like I was writing something that didn't really matter.

But as I grew up, I realized that what I was doing was actually observing the world in my own way. I started to understand that looking at things differently was not strange, but special. I find meaning in simple things and see beauty in everyday life. Whether it's a place, an object, or a moment, I draw inspiration from everything around me. Life is full of ups and downs, growth and change, and I try to capture it all in my poems.

This book is a journey of how I learned to embrace my thoughts and turn them into poetry. Each poem holds a piece of my heart, reflecting my experiences, feelings, and dreams—feelings that serve as food for thought, nourishing the mind and soul.

Acknowledgements

I am deeply grateful to everyone who has supported me on this journey. To my loving partner, thank you for your unwavering belief in me and for encouraging me to keep writing, even when I doubted myself. To my parents, your endless support and sacrifices have shaped me into the person I am today—I am forever grateful for your faith in me. To my sister, your constant presence and understanding have been a source of strength and comfort.

I also want to thank my friends and well-wishers who have inspired me with their kind words and encouragement. Your support has given me the confidence to share my thoughts with the world. Finally, to every reader who picks up this book, thank you for allowing my words to become a part of your world. I hope they resonate with you as much as they have with me.

1. Penning My Thoughts

Writing my thoughts feels like therapy,
Like I'm letting go, setting myself free.
A random thought, a fleeting sight,
Turns into words that feel just right.

As I pen them down, it feels like magic,
Sometimes overwhelming, sometimes nostalgic.
I even ask myself—
Is it really me who thinks this way?
The same me who once believed,
These thoughts were silly, a waste of the day?

Should I use this time instead,
To memorize formulas, fill my head?
Learn from books, score good marks,
And chase a future with rigid sparks?

I was a kid with low esteem,
No worth, no hope, just a fading dream.
Believed I'd never achieve a thing,
Live my life as nobody—just drifting.

But now my words, they speak so loud,
They lift me up, they make me proud.

With every line, I feel it grow,
The part of me I didn't know.

So here I write, with heart in hand,
No more doubts, I understand.
Each word I pen, each thought I say,
Tells me I am more than yesterday.

2. My Own Standard

I've changed my path, year by year,
Exploring multiple domains, my heart clear.
People said I lacked focus, a wandering soul,
But I gained experience, and wisdom made me whole.

I learned and grew, with each new day,
No regrets, just joy, in every step of the way.
I savoured each moment, in comfort and in peace,
My work a source of happiness, my heart's release.

Doubts crept in, with passing years,
"Am I accomplished enough?" through laughter and
tears.
But I never regretted, my choices, my pace,
For I knew my worth, in this corporate space.

My parents asked, with concern and care,
"Have you been promoted?" with siblings' achievements
to share.
But I'm happy for them, in their own success,
For me, it's moderation, my own happiness.

I don't strive for exceptional, nor underperform,
Meeting expectations, my own standard to form.

I enjoy my corporate life, with balance and with ease,
My bare minimum, a choice, not a compromise, if you
please.

This is my story, my journey, my way,
A path of self-discovery, day by day.

3. It's Okay to Be Me

Sometimes I feel alone, even in a crowd,
Feeling lost, and not allowed.
But in this quiet, my thoughts are loud,
In this space, my dreams are found.

I may not be someone's first choice,
But I know I have my own voice.
In my heart, I make some noise,
I am special, that's my rejoice.

So, I'm okay with being alone,
It's a time when my true self is shown.
I am important, it's widely known,
In my life, I have grown.

Remember, it's okay to feel this way,
Many people do, every single day.
In life's journey, as we sway,
We become stronger, come what may.

So here's to you, standing strong,
Where you truly belong.

4. Want to be like a Tree

In every season, come what may,
Like a tree, I wish to sway.
Offering shade, cool and wide,
No matter who, or what's inside.

In every season, steadfast and tall,
The tree stands, offering shade to all.
Its branches stretch, embracing the sky,
A sheltering haven, never asking why.

With roots deep in the earth's embrace,
I'll stand firm, with unyielding grace.
Through sun and storm, I'll endure,
A shelter for all, steadfast and pure.

But alas, for humans, it's not the same,
With hearts and minds, we bear the flame.
We feel and think, in joy and pain,
Unlike the tree, we can't refrain

Human hearts, they feel too much,
In joy and sorrow, they can't clutch.
Though I long to be as free,
My heart and mind define me.

5. Entwined Paths

Two rivers meet, between mountains high
Different paths, yet they touch the sky
One clear, one dark, their colors blend
As they flow together, a new journey to mend

Mountains watch, with a curious eye
Each one thinking, "The other river changed the sky"
But rivers know, as they flow and grow
Their paths entwined, a new story to show

We're like the rivers, ever-changing and free
Meeting, merging, and growing wild and carefree
Others may watch, from the mountainside
But we must know, our own hearts' tide

6. Beyond the Bars

In our cage, we sit and stare,
Watching creatures roam, without a care.
We claim to love safaris, to see them run wild,
But do they feel safe, or a need to hide?

They cherish freedom, yet fear what we can't see,
As we gaze at their world, so vast and carefree.
We value our own space, our right to be alone,
But forget they too have lives of their own.

Let's respect their feelings, their lands so wide,
And give them the privacy we hold inside.

7. In the Skies, We Rise

Through the airplane window, I gazed down below,
Watching as people and houses slowly faded from view.
As we climbed higher, the noise slipped away,
Replaced by calm skies and the soft light of day.

And then it struck me: perhaps life is the same,
When we grow tall enough, free from others' claims.
When we stop caring what others might say,
Their thoughts and judgments drift far away.

Rising above, their words lose their might,
Their voices and presence fall out of sight.
No longer bound by what others believe,
We find in the silence the courage to breathe.

So let us ascend, shedding fears we've outgrown,
Leaving behind all that once felt true.
For high in the heavens, with peace in our eyes,
We find our true selves in the endless blue skies.

8. Whispers of a Rainy Night

Standing on the balcony, lost in thought,
I watch people walking, some by car, some on foot.
Horns blare, kids call out to their moms,
One street, many stories, many concerns.

The drizzle begins, and they hurry home,
The once-busy street now silent, a different tone.
Mothers call their children back inside,
As rain replaces the hustle, thundering far and wide.

Blinking streetlights, thunder's roar,
A quiet night has begun, the bustle before.
The crowded, chaotic street begins to clear,
Turning into a silent, empty road, still and near.

What was once alive with bustling feet,
Now lies still beneath the rain's steady beat.

9. A Lesson from the Sea

Standing on the shore, I gazed out at the tide,
The vastness of the ocean, a sight to abide.
The waves and their soothing sound, a calming peace to share,
A bond that connected me, to the rhythm of the air.

As I walked along the beach, serenity filled my soul,
But suddenly, a bottle hit me, and my peace was stole.
I turned to see what happened, and realized with a sigh,
Someone had thrown something, and the sea had returned it to the sky.

Just like the ocean, we take things for granted, it's true,
But the sea doesn't keep what's not its own, it returns it anew.
All creatures have a limit to their patience, don't you see,
The ocean's vastness is like a big heart, generous and free.

It takes the colour of the sky, and gives back water in the form of clouds,
A give-and-take policy, where moderation is allowed.
Though the ocean gives salt water, the sky returns sweet, drinkable rain,

A balance that's maintained, a harmony that's sustained.

Let's learn from the ocean and the sky, how they manage and rely,
A lesson in balance, a tale of moderation, that touches the sky.
Hats off to their courage, hats off to their life balance, too,
A reminder to appreciate, the beauty that's shared by me and you.

10. Beyond the Moonlit Dreams

As a kid, I always used to chase moon,
Thinking one fine day I will be able to grab or move ahead soon.
Immature mind, but was thoughtful,
Poet in me was observing like nobody else can.

That imagination never happened, obviously,
But as innocence faded and mind became mature gradually.
Now I know how it works and the science behind it too,
But the art about it got slowly fade, with nothing to pursue.

Even now, as adult, I chase the dreams,
Thinking one fine day I will be able to grab it or move ahead of it, it seems.
Now the mind is mature and even thoughtful,
Poet in me still is observing, with emotions insightful.

And this imagination slowly is happening,
And as I'm growing and days I'm achieving, with heart still expanding.
Now I know how it works and science behind it,

The art is also as alive as it should be, intertwined within it.

11. The City of My Birth

The city where my life's story began,
A crown that always fits just right on this earth I've
planned.
Each return feels like stepping into the world anew,
Nostalgia wraps around me, regret for having left you.

In this city, surrounded by ocean's waves so blue,
The fast-paced life of finance, a capital that's unmatched,
shines through.
No city in the country can match its might,
The finance capital, a hub that's always in sight.

Being here is a heavenly escape, like a Friday's delight,
The warmth fills my heart, heavy with the thought of
departure's night.
Yet, there's a sense of anticipation, as if I'm a treat to be
savored,
You might guess where I am from, without much drama,
unaltered.

My heart's overwhelmed, eyes brimming with pain,
Not exaggeration, just sorrow to sustain.
A glimpse of where my childhood was shared,
Neither person nor place, yet my feelings are bared.

The place and the person don't feel the same,
My tears flowed, yet neither knows my name.
I'll return with joy, for someone loving awaits,
Love you dearly, though my heart aches.

12. Bella Ciao

Thinking of leaving, it gives heartache,
Never felt I'd have so much to take.
Overwhelmed in this moment, can't say goodbye,
Words catch in my throat, though I try not to cry.

Lots of respect, this place deserved,
It's tough to express all the feelings I've reserved.
So hard to say farewell—Bella Ciao, intertwined,
A bittersweet goodbye, forever on my mind.

Hello, Bengaluru, your warmth is a balm,
I return with a heart that seeks your calm.
Finding the courage to write is a fight,
Yet your welcoming spirit makes everything right.

In one, I was born, in the other, I thrived,
Seen ups and downs, both cities survived.
Both wear a crown, both deserved renown,
How much I speak, feelings won't subside, memories
savoured somehow.

13. A Lesson Learned

I remember as a kid, afraid to open my mouth
Scared to speak to people, my feelings locked without
A voice to express, anger or pain
My emotions hidden, like autumn's leaves in rain

Yet when it came to siblings or friends in need
I was first to support, indeed
But always, always, I got the backstabbing pain
A gift I didn't want, a lesson in vain

I wanted to be responsible, a good daughter, sister true
But in the race of being all this, I lost myself, anew
At the end, I couldn't face my own self, regrets abound
Why did I do it for others, but not for myself, a wound?

Nobody from that time is here for me now
Nobody means nobody, not a single soul somehow
Not a single human to say "you were there for me"
Even when I was there for you, a painful memory

Now I've passed this phase long ago
Sharing it because I've learned to let go
Do help others, but not before yourself, take heed
Get your things done, respect all, but set boundaries with

speed

Have courage to say no, don't be afraid to refuse
For being there always, when others can take care of
themselves, it's time to choose.

14. A Stubborn Girl

In the world of dreams, she stands so tall,
A stubborn girl with dreams so grand and all.
Her face, a canvas filled with light,
Glowing with hopes that feel so right.

She's bold, she's strong, she dares to fly,
Chasing dreams, reaching high.
But deep inside, where no one sees,
Harsh words can shake her with such ease.

She's like a mountain, standing still,
A shining star with unbent will.
Yet in her heart, so soft, so free,
Lies a melody, quiet as can be.

Harsh words may come, like winter's cold,
But still, she blooms, brave and bold.
She's a story, a song, an untold tale,
A stubborn girl who will not fail.

Her charm shines bright, soft and true,
A little light to guide you through.
So speak with love, don't make it rough,
Because deep inside, she feels enough.

15. A Couple

They argue, they fight, but they stay side by side,
Holding on through every rough tide.
Words may hurt, and tempers may rise,
But their love is real, no need for disguise.

When things get hard and times are tough,
They don't give up—they stay strong enough.
They may argue, they may not agree,
But their love is clear for all to see.

It's not always easy, not always smooth,
But their love stays strong, tried and true.
They don't always get things right,
Yet somehow, they find the light.

So here's to the couple who laugh and fight,
Loving each other with all their might.
Through every high and every low,
Their love's the one thing sure to grow.

16. From Noise to Voice

In childhood, I lacked motivation's fire,
Never thought about my future's desire.
One day, in class, I read aloud with a husky tone,
My classmates laughed, but my teacher made me feel at home.

She stopped them and said, "You can be a teacher, don't you know?"
"And you, just noise." Her words sparked a glow.
I thought, "I'll study hard and prove her right,"
But life doesn't always go as planned, day and night.

I wasn't great at academics, nor did I have a hidden flair,
No one noticed my strengths, or so it seemed, without a care.
But life took a turn, and I started to earn and learn,
Worked as a teacher while still in college, my journey to discern.

Like the moon, I grew, slowly but surely, phase by phase,
From teaching to corporate, my career path amazed.
I moved on, gradually, leaving the past behind,
Now it's time to focus on my passion, and make it shine.

17. Dreams

Dreams, they say, aren't what you see in sleep,
But what keeps you awake, your heart does keep.
I'm struggling to make my dreams come true,
Sipping my favourite brew, thinking it through.

Dreaming is easy, but fulfilment's tough,
Rough roads to destination, enough to get rough.
Goosebumps and tears won't suffice, I must confess,
Taking a step ahead, embracing change, I must address.

My dreams are small nowadays, a tiny curve I chase,
But bigger dreams await, a trigger to set the pace.
I yearn to dream so much that sleep becomes a distant
past,
And dreams become my friends, forever to last.

Now I understand, the quote that once inspired,
Dreams aren't sleepy visions, but what keeps your heart
fired.

18. The Key to Success

Success shines bright as the morning sun,
Achieving it requires getting burned, the journey's just
begun.
Determination is key, with persuasion it's won,
Desire it deeply, aim high, and success will be done.

Risk is essential, brisk efforts required each day,
Ambition's the first step, action follows, come what may.
Believe in yourself, create your own path,
Enthusiasm and intellectualism, a winning math.

Patience is vital, brilliance unfolds with time,
Success can't be rushed, overnight achievements sublime.
Acquire it slowly, and your decisions will be bright,
Success, a journey, not a destination, shining with
delight.

19. Smiling Through It All

I smile when happy, smile when blue
Smile in the rain, smile thinking of you
Smile in pain, smile when life's unfair
Smile in the mirror, smile without a care

Smile after mistakes, smile with a few friends true
Smile in success, smile in defeat, too
Smile when I win, smile when I lose
Smile with desire, smile with heart that chooses

I smile for love that's always near
Filling my heart with joy, calming my fear.

20. Patience Pays Off

Patience pays off better, it's a virtue true,
Not just a word to say, but a principle to pursue.
Obey its wisdom, and you'll find it's worth the wait,
For patience, though bitter, yields a sweeter fate.

With patience, the impossible becomes achievable too,
A sign of capability, shining bright and anew.
Impatience can never taste success's sweet delight,
For only patience makes a person flawless, shining
bright.

Patience takes time, sometimes late, but don't despair,
The fruit of patience is worthy of the wait, beyond
compare.
Patience never brings regret, only peace of mind,
Control anxiety and fret, leave patience to unwind.

Patience tests can be terrible, but results are grand,
Honourable outcomes await, in this patient land.
Patience isn't just waiting, it's how you react while you
wait,
A mindset of calm and trust, a heart that's patient and
great.

21. Self-Love, Self-Respect

If loving myself first is being mean,
Then yes, I'm guilty, my heart's serene.
If living life on my terms is selfish too,
Then yes, I'm selfish, my dreams I pursue.

If prioritizing self-respect is egoistic pride,
Then yes, I'm egoistic, my dignity I provide.
If not caring for others' opinions is apathetic cold,
Then yes, I'm apathetic, my heart no longer sold.

If speaking my mind without filters is being rude,
Then yes, I'm rude, my truth I choose to produce.
If not apologizing for feelings I don't regret,
Then yes, I'm arrogant, my self-worth I won't forget.

If showing anger at misbehaviour is hatred's fire,
Then yes, I'm hateful, injustice I desire to retire.
If following my heart, doing what I want to do,
Then yes, I'm a rebel, my freedom I pursue.

22. Rise Above the Pain

They wearied of our tears, and turned away from pain
But our smiles remained, a mask to hide the strain
Those who inflicted hurt, and gave us sorrow's might
We drank it in, and suffered through the dark of night

We bore the brunt alone, with no one to share the blame
Neither here nor there, we felt no sense of shame
We thought we'd rise above, and make a brand new start
Move forward, and leave the heartache deep in our heart

We need a purpose now, a reason to carry on
A desire to rise above, and shine like the morning sun
We need to focus tight, and let go of the past
No more lingering, no more looking back at all

Now we live for ourselves, for our own sake and pride
Moving forward, with hearts that are healing inside.

23. Lost in Thought

I'm not happy nor sad
Just stuck in this space
Thinking about what I had
What I was, what I've been

If only I had a magic stick
I'd learn all the tricks
Take back the days that slipped away
Hold on to them till my dying day

Those days gave me strength and tears
Thinking about them still fills me with fears

Life's a game that taunts and teases
Laughs and cries in every phases
A maze, a test, a trial by fire
But we must live it, with heart and desire

24. I Never Thought

25. Unfulfilled Longings

Some things are beyond our control
Some desires never fade or grow old
We thought we'd live life with a carefree heart
Drinking in the sorrows, playing our part

We've forgiven, but we'll never forget
Will we ever turn our dreams into reality we've met?
People played with our emotions, it's true
We're still living with the longing, feeling blue

Our hearts are tired of crying, it's time to move on
It doesn't matter who's around, our hearts are still strong
Every breath reminds us of those memories past
When our own people pointed fingers, and our trust
didn't last

There's nothing left to lose, no more tears to cry
All we need is a shroud to wrap our weary eyes

26. Unspoken Emotions

I wish I could cry, let go and be free
But tears are dry, and emotions locked in me
I'm searching for someone who understands my pain
Waiting to laugh with glee, and love again

I'm speechless, feeling overwhelmed and blue
No need for healing, just someone to see me through
They say they care, but words are just empty space
I need a break from this world, a hiding place

The weight of past and present pain is crushing me
I'm resentful, tired of pretending to be free
Everyone claims to understand, but can't walk the mile
I'm faking smiles, hiding tears, all the while

People don't grasp what's inside, they just talk and hide
Unanswered questions linger, who, what, why, and when
to decide
No one notices dry tears, I need to break the mold
Why can't I cry? Emotions dried, growing old

But when appreciated and motivated, I feel strong and
new
With emotions overflowing, I smile, and see this journey

through
Tears bring sympathy, smiles bring confidence, I've
found
I'll wear my smile, my confidence, my heart's renowned

My love, strength, and confidence come from within
My smile, my audience, my heart's kin
I love and care for myself, I'm my own best friend
Together, we'll journey on, until the very end.

27. Scattered Pearls

The day was awesome, everything fine,
Enjoyed each moment, including dine.
But then my thoughts took a strange turn,
Everything felt same, my feelings yearned.

I'm lost, unsure if I'm happy or blue,
Days seem cheerful, nights still dark and new.
I think of myself, or others too,
End up caring deeply, with emotions anew.

Friends see me as daring, caring and bright,
Family confused, seeing both day and night.
Relatives, nowhere to be found,
My original self, lost in dreams unbound.
I'm confused, unsure, or maybe obscure,
Longing to find my true self, pure.

My dreams were simple, but scattered wide,
Like pearls that fell, and can't be tied.
I'm searching for a string to make them whole,
A necklace to wear, with a story to unfold.

Can someone guide me, on where to roam?
To find the threads that'll make my dreams a home?

I don't want to chase, the scattered pearls alone,
But create many necklaces, with a heart that's made of
stone.
35

I may not understand, but I have faith anew,
One day, life will curve, and my heart will renew.
No more confusion, no more happy or blue,
Days and nights will shine, with a heart that's true.

28. Space to Breathe

Good morning, good evening, good night
These words sound very light tonight
Need to think to say it or mean it
But the time is playing with it

Why these people are behind me
Trying to teach me, but annoying me
Tried my best to avoid you, I confess
But I don't have patience anymore, I must profess

Will try each and every possible way
So that I can decide before my hairs turn grey
Leave me alone, give me space to be
I don't need your guidance, just let me be me

In silence, I'll search for my own way
Through life's challenges, come what may
Will try to find my inner voice, my heart's beat
And discover peace, where love and calm meet.

29. The Choice of Happiness

Happiness is a choice, choose it every day
It is what you think and what you say
I want it today as well as tomorrow
So that there's no chance of sorrow

The key to happiness is in my pocket
I want to fly with it in a rocket
It is an inside job
The feeling that no one can rob

May this day give you lots of happiness that lasts
forever?
Sorrows and grief shouldn't touch you ever
May all your wishes come true?
And happiness always be with you

May joy and love surround you each day?
And happiness be your guide on the way
May all your dreams and hopes come true?
And happiness forever shine through.

30. A Wishful Heart

Wish we were what we thought we'd be
Every dream of ours would come true, effortlessly
Our desire to live would grow stronger each day
When magic happens, and our hearts find a way

Wish there were no heartaches or sorrowful nights
We'd keep smiling till our last shining lights
If we couldn't do anything else in life's pace
At least we'd learn to live, and find our own space

Wish we could turn back time, and change the past
Learn to love without fear, and let go of hatred at last
Life's strange phase has brought us to a place
Where love's been discarded, and hatred's taken its space

Wish we could learn what love truly means to share
Then we'd surely write that heartbreak's a curse to bear

31. Conditionally Blessed

I'm the firstborn, oh so serene,
Thanks to my parents, who made me the experiment
scene.
Their first experience, full of love and delight,
A charm that shone so bright, but also a little
frightening.

Not their mistake, just their first try,
Everybody's happy, until the next sibling comes by.
No complaints, no regrets, just a gift from above,
A middle-class family, with limited options, but endless
love.

They unwrapped the gift, without a price tag to pay,
Couldn't afford to preserve, but made do every step of
the way.
Lucky me, got wings to fly, but with conditions, of
course,
Moderation, values, and concerns, but also a dash of
force.

People talk, without a clue,
Controlling, judging, with nothing to do.
Born as a woman, a whole different ball game,

You'd never know, until you wear the same.

Men have their struggles, their plates full and wide,
But they can say no, walk out, with a sense of pride.
Women, on the other hand, must stay, must obey,
Their expressions, their voices, often silenced, day by
day.

So here's to being born first, with a dash of luck,
A middle-class family, with love that's stuck.
I'll take the wings, with conditions, and all,
But also the knowledge, that I'll never fall.

32. Choosing Peace, but not Silence

One random day, I was thinking deep,
"What if I choose peace, and arguments sleep?"
What if I choose peace, over every discussion and fray?
What if I choose peace, and don't bother with my
thoughts each day?

But then I realized, if everybody chose peace too,
The world would miss out on innovation, and all we'd do.
No medicines to cure diseases, no breakthroughs to
share,
No great achievements, as we'd be choosing peace,
without a care.

If we all chose peace, without questioning or debate,
We'd miss out on the genius of minds that create and
participate.
Anybody before being a big shot, is a normal human
with a view,
It's their nature to question, which gives them
understanding, and helps them break through.

So we shouldn't say, "Don't question the elders," or "Keep
quiet, it's not your place,"

Instead, we should think, "How can we help you shine, and bring your ideas to the space?"

33. The Illusion of Peace

I know the crowd will shout, "Peace is not silence, it's a
choice we make!"
But I say, if we really mean it, it's not just a word we
undertake.
Keeping peace in today's world means keeping quiet,
pretending all is well,
Don't question the obvious results, or you'll be labelled a
pessimist to tell.

But if you don't question, you're not confident, or so they
say,
You're not capable, just a follower, living life in a world
of gray.
I've lived both lives, with experience as my guide,
And I've found that judging others leads to the same
result, side by side.

It's those in power who want you to be their puppet, just
like they were before,
But choosing to live on your own terms, that's what
peace is looking for.
Peace is something we feel within, not something
someone else can define,

It's a sense of calm, a sense of self, that's truly one of a
kind.

34. The Perfectionism Trap

Brought up in a family where discipline, manners,
timeliness was the key to live life,
As I was around them, similar thoughts grew up and had
the same perspective in strife.
You know the say, we become, as we surround to be
with, in every life,
At some extent, it helped a lot to be consistent and tidy
on the task, no need to think twice.

But it triggered when I was out from this robotic
behaviour, so free,
I was enjoying any moment, just to be a perfectionist,
that's just me.
I know that each has flaws on its own, as they have, we
can, we do have none, it's plain to see,
They being perfect made them strict and rude, not a trait
I'd want to be.

Even those are not good traits, that's for sure,
Because I have seen people success with being cool, and
that's what I'd endure.
Perfectionism ruins the living in the day, in every way,
It's a lesson I've learned, to live life in a better way.

35. A Life of Change, A Life of Growth

With time, I learnt we don't have same people in all our times,
From school to start working, being kid to be adult we change people in all levels and phases that chime.
At times we like certain crowd and other times we have different choice,
And there will be a time a person replica of yours you may not like, a different voice.

So we should know how to embrace the change, respect others too,
Try to be mindful and respectful in giving back, that's what we do.
As we all know it, we will get it back, in every single way,
That's the law of life, come what may.

Someone once said to me, "Do you have one human you can call friend?"
Still, though I was not allowed to make friends, because of the discipline we carry with us that never end.
But now those words sound dumb, I've moved on, I've grown,

I had friends in all phases of my life, never same, but lessons were shown.
I changed, they changed, we evolved, and so did the world, it's true,
That's the journey of life, with friendships old and new.